M*A*P
(MEN AGAINST PORN)

How to Break the Chains

James Spooner

WestBow
PRESS
A DIVISION OF THOMAS NELSON

NIV—Scripture taken from the Rainbow Study Bible Copyright 1981. Used with permission from Standard Publishing Company. All rights reserved.

WestBow Press books may be ordered through booksellers or by contacting:

WestBow Press
A Division of Thomas Nelson
1663 Liberty Drive
Bloomington, IN 47403
www.westbowpress.com
1-(866) 928-1240

ISBN: 978-1-4497-7724-1 (sc)
ISBN: 978-1-4497-7725-8 (hc)
ISBN: 978-1-4497-7723-4 (e)

Library of Congress Control Number: 2012922481

Printed in the United States of America

WestBow Press rev. date: 11/28/2012

ARMOR OF GOD

Finally, be strong in the Lord and in his mighty power. Put on the full armor of God so that you can take your stand against the devil's schemes. For our struggle is not against flesh and blood, but against the rulers, against the authorities, against the powers of this dark world and against the spiritual forces of evil in the heavenly realms. Therefore put on the full armor of God, so that when the day of evil comes, you may be able to stand your ground, and after you have done everything, to stand. Stand firm then, with the **belt of truth** buckled around your waist, with the **breastplate of righteousness** in place, and with your feet fitted with the readiness that comes from the gospel of peace. In addition to all this take up the **shield of faith**, with which you can extinguish all the flaming arrows of the evil one. Take the **helmet of salvation** and the **sword of the spirit**, which is the word of God. And pray in the Spirit on all occasions with all kinds of prayers and request. "(emphasis added)"

Ephesians 6:10–18

To my beloved wife, who God has anointed her with unconditional love for her husband—me!

And to those women whose husbands are still held in chains by this addiction. I implore you to stay the course with your husbands; we are all God's children, and sometimes we get wounded. If a child came to you and was cut, would you not clean the wound and place a bandage on it to help start the healing process? This study is meant to help in the healing process along with God's Word.

CONTENTS

M*A*P

INTRODUCTION

Men *Against Porn* (*MAP*) is an intense twelve-week study guide designed for men addicted to pornography or other forms of sexual immorality. This program helps break those chains that bind them to this worldly epidemic. Right from the beginning, you will be immersed with confronting your addiction through intense communication guided by God's love for you as written in His Scripture. That is right—God's Word takes a huge part in our healing process.

God put this study on my heart to design it in a way that it uses 99 percent Scripture and 1 percent of my personal testimony. That's what makes this study unique—using mostly God's Word to heal us. I feel the use of numerical statistics does not help in that healing process and only gives us information from surveys. Don't get me wrong; there are other study guides on the subject of pornography addiction that are indeed very helpful. For example, *Breaking Free* by Russell Willingham and *The Bondage Breaker* by Neil T. Anderson. But in my opinion, they are not intense enough from the start.

Now is the time to break those chains and grow in the Lord our God through grace, faith, and in His unconditional love for us.

For men who want to venture on the path of freeing themselves from pornography addiction, this will be an in-your-face study that confronts subjects men normally don't want to talk about, because they are embarrassed, they are afraid, they are angry, or they demonstrate many other symptoms that stem from the chains of pornography.

You must want to do this weekly study for yourself and for God; if you are here because someone else wanted you to attend this course; you are here for all the wrong reasons and need to come back when you are ready.

I assure you that what we talk about in class stays within this study group and classroom, but I do encourage you to openly communicate to your wife if you are married. Believe me—your marriage will become the best it's ever been.

COVENANT

The Lord gave us a new covenant in the New Testament, and in this new covenant He states, "For I will forgive their wickedness and will remember their sins no more" (Hebrews 8:12). God loves us so much that he not only forgives us but also forgets our sins.

You must agree to completely open your heart, mind, and soul to God and to this study. Remember, you are safe here. Just because we are men does not mean we can't have emotions. You will laugh and cry, and we will pray together.

This covenant you are about to make is vitally important to the success of breaking those chains of addiction to pornography. If you are not in in total agreement with this study, (come back when you are ready). Please read the following, and then sign your name.

I am committed to honoring Jesus Christ through worship, prayer, and obedience to God's Word in the power of the Holy Spirit. To pursue vital relationships with a few other men understanding the need of accountability. To stay committed to practicing spiritual, moral, ethical, and sexual purity. To build strong marriages and families through love, protection and biblical values.

Your Signature: _____

Date: _____

    This covenant is a requirement for men who want to start their journey in breaking the chains that bind us to this sin.

    Another requirement is that you bring your Bible to every class. You are allowed to miss only one class, because if you miss two or more classes, you lose focus on the goal of breaking away from pornography. You must take this seriously, for your life depends on it, and so does God. If you feel that this class is too intense at this time, I suggest attending another class at your church that would still aid in dealing with your sexual integrity!

ABOUT THE AUTHOR

My name is James Spooner, and I am addicted to pornography. It started when I was twelve years old when my father brought home porn magazines like *Playboy* and *Penthouse*; he even had 8mm pornography films hidden in his closet.

The moment I saw those pictures and films, Satan grabbed me and never let go—or at the least he never completely let me go.

Now let's jump many years ahead, to my great late forties. I was still addicted to porn. I almost lost my marriage because I was into Internet pornography and hiding it from my wife, and I was also trying hard to hide it from God. Then one day at church, Pastor Jim Garlow was preaching to me even though there were hundreds in the Saturday-night service. I felt God's hands upon my shoulders, and he spoke to me for the first time on my sin of porn. He put upon my heart *MAP*, *Men Against Porn*. This is a journey that I believe God has planned for me on the pathway to becoming closer to him and to help other men who are struggling to break free from the chains of this addiction. It is still a daily fight to not accept the temptation that our society so openly puts in my pathways, or should I say that Satan puts in front of me to get me to fall away from God. I pray every day that God puts his grace, love, and his armor around me to help me stay away from this addition of pornography. Throughout this journey, you will hear more of my encounters with this addiction as well as other men's testimonies, in the hopes that you will be able to relate and gain encouragement to break your chains of pornography.

Contact Info:
Cell: 951–816–9302
E-mail: golferspoons44@hotmail.com

ACCOUNTABILITY PARTNERS

This is the beginning of the end of your journey to breaking the chains of porn addiction. At this time, please pick at least three accountability partners (APs) from this class. Exchange phone numbers, e-mails, and addresses. This is the start of your intense accountability, which is a major factor in this study. Please put your accountability partners' information below so you have a handy reference to contact them at any time.

To all accountability partners: it is your responsibility to contact your APs *twice a week* to hold them accountable to this study, to their families, to themselves, and to God. Please print clearly.

Name: _____ Phone: _____

E-mail: _____

Name: _____ Phone: _____

E-mail: _____

Name: _____ Phone: _____

E-mail: _____

It is imperative that you pick three men from this class to help you stay on the right pathway to breaking the chains of pornography. The more accountability you have, the easier it will be to break the bondage of this addiction. Accountability helps you stay on the correct path each week of this study. I implore you, don't take this lightly.

We cannot win this battle alone. "Though one may be overpowered, two can defend themselves. A cord of three strands is not quickly broken" (Ecclesiastes 4:12).

The following are questions *you must* ask your APs both days of each week throughout this study and even after you have accomplished this study. These questions will be good tools after you have broken away from pornography. Remember, we are in a daily fight to stay committed to God, family, and ourselves.

For Internet accountability, visit www.covenanteyes.com. There are others like this if you feel other sites work better for you. This keeps a non-erasable history of every website you visit and then e-mails it to two or more accountability partners of your choosing. Note: Your wife should be the first person on your accountability e-mail list.

Questions:

1). Have you been tempted in any way this week? If no, praise God out loud! Remember, it's not a sin to be tempted, but acting on the temptation is a sin.

If yes, then ask what tempted you or how you were tempted. Some different types of temptation are sinful thoughts, masturbation, computer sites, porn magazines, strip clubs, television shows you should not be viewing, etc.

2). Did you act on any temptation? If the answer is no, then praise God out loud!

If yes, ask why. Then ask what caused you to sin. And ask why you didn't call your accountability partners. As for the accountability partners, be firm but loving. Remember, we are here to hold each other accountable and help break these chains no matter how difficult it gets. Christ died on the cross for our sins; the least we can do is help one another fight against pornography.

Now is the time for prayer. If you experienced or acted on temptations of any kind, then please repeat the following prayer together and input the action that was done:

> Lord, I confess that I have participated in _____. I know it was evil and offensive in Your sight. Thank you for Your forgiveness. I renounce any and all involvement with ___, and I cancel out any and all ground that the enemy gained in my life through this activity. In Jesus' name I pray. Amen.

Now, if there were no temptations at all and no sinful acts according to God's words, then pray the following verse together:

> Dear Heavenly Father, it is Your will that I should be sanctified; that I should avoid sexual immorality; that I should learn to control my own body in a way that is holy and honorable, not in passionate lust like a heathen who does not know God. For you, Lord, did not call us to be impure, but to live a holy life. I pray this in Jesus' name. Amen.

It is written, "'As surely as I live,' says the Lord, 'every knee will bow before me; every tongue will confess to God.' So then, each of us will give an account of himself to God" (Romans 14:11–12). "But I tell you that men will have to give account on the Day of Judgment for every careless word they have spoken. For by your words you will be acquitted, and by your words you will be condemned" (Matthew 12:36–37).

So, men, we all must be honest and truthful toward God, our wives, our family, and our accountability partners every day of every week of every month. Remember, you are not alone on this journey.

> For the word of God is living and active. Sharper than any double-edged sword, it penetrates even to dividing soul and spirit, joints and marrow; it judges the thoughts and attitudes of the heart. Nothing in all creation is hidden from God's sight. Everything is uncovered and laid bare before the eyes of him to whom we must give account. (Hebrews 3:12–13)

JOURNEY ONE

This is the most important step you will take, and possibly the hardest step for some, if not all of you. Remember, if God is for us, who can be against us?

Statement of Truth

> I believe that God demonstrated His own love for me in that while I was still a sinner, Christ died for me. I believe that He has delivered me from the domain of darkness and transferred me to His kingdom, and in Him I have redemption, the forgiveness of sins. (See Romans 5:8; Colossians 1:13, 14.)

Please stand and read "Journey One: Admit" out loud:

Journey One: Admit

> I admit I am powerless. I'm now going to understand that I have spiritual authority over this evilness; my life

has become unmanageable. And I am here to seek God's love, grace, forgiveness, strength, and accountability.

So now that you are admitting that you are powerless over this addiction, I praise you for taking this first step. Remember, God loves you the same as anyone on this earth.

Now let's discuss this addiction and start your journey to breaking those chains off your wrists and shoulders.

Where did you first encounter porn? _____

_____

How did you feel when you first viewed porn? _____

_____

How old were you at that time? _____

_____

What about now?

How do you feel now about the first time you encountered porn?

_____

How do you feel now when you view porn?

_____

Why do you view porn at your current age?

_____

What drives your addition to porn? Satan, evil, Beelzebub?

_____

In the beginning, Adam and Eve fell to the reasoning of the serpent (Satan) in the garden of Eden, as depicted in Genesis 3:1–7. Satan's first and foremost strategy is deception. Satan does a wonderful job hiding lies within partial truths to get us to follow what is not truth at all. In 2 Corinthians 11:14–15, we read, "And no wonder, for Satan himself masquerades as an angel of light. It is not surprising, then, if his servants masquerade as servants of righteousness. Their end will be what their actions deserve."

Here are some potential *hazards* caused by pornography that Satan wants you to experience. Discuss these out loud and take notes.

- craving porn intensely and persistently
- difficulty controlling thoughts, exposure to, and use of porn
- inability to discontinue porn use despite the consequences
- repeated failures to stop using porn
- requiring extreme content or exposure to porn to get the effect (habituation symptoms)
- experiencing discomfort and irritability when deprived of porn (withdrawal symptoms)

Notes:

_____

_____

_____

_____

_____

_____

_____

_____

_____

_____

_____

Now let's tackle the question, how do you start each day fighting against this spiritual challenge?

Getting rid of computers and magazines will not solve this problem or even help with your addiction. Starting and ending your days in reading Scripture, praying, and putting on the armor of God is a good beginning. But you must make a daily commitment to doing this no matter how much you feel it's a pain or a waste of time or thinking that God won't let you into heaven because of it. That is just Satan telling you more lies. Remember what Romans 8:31–32 says: "If God is for us, who can be against us? He who did not spare his own Son, but gave him up for us all—how will he not also, along with him, graciously give us all things?"

Homework:

Please read the following Scriptures for next week's class:

1. 2 Corinthians 4:16–18
2. Isaiah 41:10–14
3. 2 Corinthians 5:6–10
4. 2 Corinthians 6:15–18

Reminder: start and end each day with the Armor of God prayer in Ephesians 6:10–19.

JOURNEY TWO

D iscuss last week's homework.

Statement of Truth

> By faith, I choose to be filled with the Spirit so that I can
> be guided into all truth. I choose to walk by the Spirit
> so that I will not carry out the desires of the flesh. (See
> John 16:13; Galatians 5:16; Ephesians 5:18.)

<u>Journey Two:</u> Fears

I admit to God and others the exact nature of my fears.

We must take responsibility for our choices, no matter how
embarrassing they might be, for as the end result, you will prevail,
standing firm with your belt of truth supporting you in ways you can't
imagine yet.

You had the free will to allow yourself to become addicted to porn;
use that same free will to stand up and admit to the wrong choices made
and face all of your fears that manifested from this addiction.

You did have help in your wrong choices, and his name is Satan. He is the great deceiver, and he will do whatever it takes to make you sin against God. He works undercover at all costs to take you down, for if he gets to you, he gets to God.

Why do we have such fears in admitting to others, such as our wives, friends, family members, and, yes, even God, that we have an addiction to porn?

Let's take a look at fear!

Deuteronomy 6:13: "Fear the Lord your God, serve him only and take your oaths in his name."

"Now all has been heard; here is the conclusion of the matter: Fear God and keep his commandments; for this is the whole duty of man. For God will bring every deed into judgment; including every hidden thing whether it is good or evil" (Ecclesiastes 12:13–14).

This prevailing fear had its origin in early human history when the choice was made to become self-directed and eliminate the purity of God's Holy Spirit and the incredible wisdom and counsel that accompanies it. This choice is described metaphorically in Genesis 3:6 as eating from "the tree of knowledge of good and evil." Immediately after the choice to abandon God's Spirit, Adam hid—the first fearful behavior described in the Bible.

When we fall to pornography, do we not feel ashamed? When we give in to our desires using pornography, are we not sinning against God And in doing so, do we not become fearful of getting caught?

Fear dilutes perfect love as well. Thus we may subliminally reject God's full measure of grace because we see ourselves as undeserving. The more we reject love—a verb, not an emotion—the more we depend on resources and intellect for survival. We search for ways to fill an empty "God-shaped" void with worldly beliefs or possessions. A vicious circle is created until we mentally crash.

We risk becoming fear driven and too dependent on resources, abilities, and intellect. We may find ourselves struggling with unethical compromise for survival in a worldly fashion as we resume old self-directive ways. We fail to realize that whomever we serve usually becomes the provider of our secondary motive, our needs.

The absence of grace, which we bring from our past or have never completely purged, may seem to work for a short period until our survival fear drives us to greed, money, power, and the typical hunger and desperate search for the five personal needs so essential to our survival: significance, security, intimacy, innocence, and hope. Self-reliance and the continual search for these five desperate needs in wrong places may even involve desires or acts of wrongful sexual behavior.

Let's discuss some of our fears listed here:

- the fear of getting caught
- the fear of telling those you love about your addiction
- the fear of letting go of your addiction
- the fear of being vulnerable
- the fear of losing your friends
- the fear of losing the pleasure this addiction gets you to believe in

What other fears do you have?

How do you deal with your fear? If it were that easy, you wouldn't be here right now! So let's go to God's Word for some guidance.

> To fear the Lord is to hate evil, I hate pride and arrogance, evil behavior and perverse speech. Counsel and sound judgment are mine; I have understanding and power. (Proverbs 8:13–14)
>
> You must hate evil, and evil behavior to get away from pornograghy.

7

The fear of the Lord is the beginning of wisdom, and knowledge of the Holy One is understanding. (Proverbs 9:10)

To gain wisdom is to fear the Lord, understanding this, but most importantly accepting this will help in your journey of breaking those chains that bind you!

I will say of the Lord, "He is my refuge and my fortress, my God, in whom I trust." (Psalm 91:2)

Instead of taking refuge in the sin of pornography, you must take refuge in God!

You will not fear the terror of night, nor the arrow that flies by day. (Psalm 91:5)

This is where you should allow the armor of God to protect you against the terror of night and the flaming arrows that satan throws at you by day.

When I am afraid, I will trust in you. In God, whose word I praise, in God I trust; I will not be afraid. What can mortal man do to me? (Psalm 56:3–4)

God is the only one that can free you from your addiction, this takes trust on your part to allow God to intercede on your behalf.

The Lord is my shepherd, I shall not be in want.

He makes me lie down in green pastures, he leads me beside quiet waters,
he restores my soul. He guides me in paths of righteousness
for his name's sake.

Even though I walk through the valley of the shadow of death, I will **fear** no evil, for you are with me your rod and your staff, they comfort me. (Psalm 23:1–4)

By trusting in the Lord, and not fearing evil, God will protect you from nightly terrors, and daily arrows that satan slings at you!

To further help strengthen your spiritual growth, as a soldier prepares for battle through a rigorous training routine, we must arm ourselves by consistently practicing spiritual disciplines. I encourage men to strengthen the warrior within with four spiritual disciplines as part of their daily routine.

1. **Read the Bible daily.** You need to get into the habit of reading the Bible each day. Start out reading for at least fifteen minutes, and then progress to longer reading times. If you find a verse that speaks to your heart, then commit it to memory.

2. **Pray.** Start each day with praying, and end each day with praying. Buy a journal and write down your prayers. As your prayers are answered, keep record of what God has done. As I have stated before, Ephesians 6:10–19 is the Armor of God prayer.

   Maintain sexual purity. If you're married, focus your thoughts on your wife. If you are not married, dwell on images that you know would please God. You control your eyes; they are the gateway through which Satan can enter.

3. **Express love to others.** If you are single, express love to family and friends. If you are married, tell your wife each day how much you love her.

   I sought the Lord, and he answered me; he delivered me from all my fears. (Psalm 34:4)

The angel of the Lord encamps around those who fear him, and he delivers them. Taste and see that the Lord is good; blessed is the man who takes refuge in him. (Psalm 34:7–8)

We wait in hope for the Lord; he is our help and our shield. (Psalm 33:20)

Homework:

Please read the following Scriptures:

1. Psalm 23
2. Psalm 18:1–3
3. Jeremiah 1:17–19
4. Luke 12:4–12
5. Ephesians 10:6–19 (the Armor of God prayer)

More of my story: When I came to another Saturday night service at Skyline Church shortly after my downfall, my pastor, Jim Garlow, whom I've known for many years now and who knew of my situation, put his hand on my shoulder and, in a very loving but firm way, stated that if I didn't come back to church that he would want to come after me and tackle me. I understood what he meant, and it melted my heart to hear that my pastor cared that much for me. So you see, there are other men that do want to help and who love you like a brother in Christ; they want for you to be set free from this addiction. You really have nothing to fear.

JOURNEY THREE

Discuss last week's homework.

Statement of Truth:

Throughout this process, you will be asking God to lead you.

He is the only one who can grant repentance leading to a knowledge of the truth, which will set you free (see 2 Timothy 2:24–26).

Journey Three: Repent

Repentance is a change of thought that is made to correct a wrong and gain forgiveness from a person who is wronged. In religious contexts, it usually refers to confession to God, ceasing sin against God, and resolving to live according to religious law. It typically includes an admission of guilt, a promise or resolution not to repeat the offense, and an attempt to make restitution for the wrong, or in some way to reverse the harmful effects of the wrong where possible.

Now let's see what the Word of God says about repenting. "Land of Zebulun and land of Naphtali, the way to the sea, along the Jorda, Galilee of the Gentiles, the people lining in darkness have seen a great light; on those living in the land of the shadow of death a light has dawned. From that time on Jesus began to preach, "Repent, for the Kingdom of heaven is near" (Matthew 4:15–17).

Jesus teaches repentance. Jesus answered, "Do you think that these Galileans were worse sinners than all the other Galileans because they suffered this way? I tell you, no! But unless you **repent**, you too will perish. Or those eighteen who died when the tower in Siloam fell on them-do you think they were more guilty than all the others living in Jerusalem? I tell you, no! But unless you **repent**, you too will all perish" (Luke 13:2—5).

God has blessed us with a healthy sexual desire, and through our addiction to pornography, we have made a mockery of this gift; we have turned it into a self-pleasurable act of sin.

> Peter replied, "**Repent** and be baptized, every one of you, in the name of Jesus Christ for the forgiveness of your sins. And you will receive the gift of the Holy Spirit. The promise is for you and your children and for all who are far off-for all whom the Lord our God will call."

> With many other words he warned them; and he pleaded with them, "Save yourselves from this corrupt generation." Those who accepted his message were baptized, and about three thousand were added to their number that day. (Acts 2:38–41)

> Therefore since we are God's offspring, we should not think that the divine being is like gold or silver or stone- an image made by man's design and skill. In the past God overlooked such ignorance, but now he commands all people everywhere to **repent**. For he has set a day

when he will judge the world with justice by the man he has appointed. He has given proof of this to all men by raising him from the dead. (Acts 17:29–31)

Besides prayer, repentance is the only honest response and the only effective way of dealing with our dark side.

Yet now I am happy, not because you were made sorry, but because your sorrow led you to **repentance**. For you became sorrowful as God intended and so were not harmed in any way by us. Godly sorrow brings **repentance** that leads to salvation and leaves no regret, but worldly sorrow brings death. (2 Corinthians 7:9–10)

In the same way, I tell you, there is rejoicing in the presence of the angels of God over one sinner who **repents**. (Luke 15:10)

So watch yourselves. "If your brother sins, rebuke him, and if he **repents**, forgive him. If he sins against you seven times in a day, and seven times comes back to you and says, 'I **repent**,' forgive him." (Luke 17:3-4)

Notes:

_____

_____

_____

_____

_____

_____

_____

We need to acquire an antidote of repentance and use it to help fight against the deceit and selfishness of this addiction.

Homework:

Please read the following Scriptures:

1. Job 42:1–6
2. Jeremiah 15:19
3. Luke 3:7–8
4. Acts 26:20

Don't forget to read Ephesians 6:10–18.

JOURNEY FOUR

Go over last week's homework.

Statement of Forgiveness:

You will start gaining freedom when you make direct amends to those people you have injured through porn. We can see an example of forgiveness in the following scripture.

"This is what you are to say to Joseph: I ask you to forgive your brothers the sins and the wrongs they committed in treating you so badly" (Genesis 50:17).

Journey Four: Forgiveness

God wants all of us to be free; and the only way to accomplish this is to be obedient to God.

> And he passed in front of Moses, proclaiming, "The Lord, the Lord, the compassionate and gracious God, slow to anger, abounding in love and faithfulness, maintaining love to thousands, and forgiving

wickedness, rebellion and sin. Yet he does not leave the guilty unpunished; he punishes the children and their children for the sin of the fathers to the third and fourth generation." (Exodus 34:6–7)

Going to the people we've hurt and asking for their forgiveness is not an easy thing to do. In fact, it's one of the hardest acts for a man to do, because we allow for pride to get in our way. We must pray and ask God to keep us humble and give us the strength we need to confront the people whose trust we have lost.

> If you, O Lord, kept a record of sins, O Lord, who could stand? But with you there is forgiveness; therefore you are feared. (Psalm 130:3–4)

> Who is a God like you, who pardons sin and forgives the transgression of the remnant of his inheritance? You do not stay angry forever but delight to show mercy. (Micah 7:18)

> Then Peter came to Jesus and asked, "Lord, how many times shall I forgive my brother when he sins against me? Up to seven times?" Jesus answered, "I tell you, not seven times, but seventy-seven times. (Matthew 18:21–22)

> If you forgive anyone, I also forgive him. And what I have forgiven-if there was anything to forgive---I have forgiven in the sight of Christ for your sake, in order that Satan might not outwit us. For we are not unaware of his schemes.
> (2 Corinthians 2:10–11)

When you were dead in your sins and in the uncircumcision of your sinful nature, God made you alive with Christ. He forgave us all our sins, having canceled the written code, with its regulations, that was against us and that stood opposed to us; he took it away, nailing it to the cross. (Colossians 2:13–14)

Get rid of all bitterness, rage and anger, brawling and slander, along with every form of malice. Be kind and compassionate to one another, forgiving each other, just as in Christ God forgave you. (Ephesians 4:31–32)

When asking for forgiveness, don't expect anything in return and don't allow yourself to become angry if the other person refuses to forgive you at that moment. Give them up to God, and let God deal with their choice of unforgiveness. Remember, you are the one who is asking for their forgiveness; we can't get caught up with their choices. You are here to get healed from pornography, and this is just one of the steps in that process. Out of forgiveness comes reconciliation, and out of reconciliation comes part of the healing process.

Therefore, if you are offering your gift at the altar and there remember that your brother has something against you; leave a gift there in front of the altar. First go and be **reconciled** to your brother; then come and offer your gift. (Matthew 5:23–24)

For he himself is our peace, who has made the two one and has destroyed the barrier, the dividing wall of hostility, by abolishing in his flesh the law with its commandments and regulations. His purpose was to create in himself one new man out of the two, thus making peace, and in this one body to **reconcile** both

17

of them to God through the cross, by which he put to death their hostility. (Ephesians 2:14–16)

Once you were alienated from God and were enemies in your minds because of your evil behavior. But now he has **reconciled** you by Christ's physical body through death to present you holy in his sight, without blemish and free from accusation. (Colossians 1:21–22)

For if, when we were God's enemies we were **reconciled** to him through the death of his Son, how much more, having been reconciled, shall we be saved through his life! Not only is this so but we also rejoice in God through our Lord Jesus Christ, through whom we have now received reconciliation. (Romans 5:10–11)

Notes:

_____

_____

_____

_____

_____

_____

_____

_____

_____

_____

_____

I said, "O Lord, have mercy on me; **heal me**, for I have sinned against you." (Psalm 41:4)

Just then a woman who had been subject to bleeding for twelve years came up behind him and touched the edge of his cloak. She said to herself, "If I only touch his cloak, I will be **healed**." Jesus turned and saw her. "Take heart, daughter," he said, "your faith has healed you." And the woman was healed from that moment. (Matthew 9:20–23)

He said, "If you listen carefully to the voice of the Lord your God and do what is right in his eyes, if you pay attention to his commands and keep all his decrees, I will not bring on you any of the diseases I brought on the Egyptians, for I am the Lord, who **heals** you." (Exodus 15:26)

Don't get discouraged if it takes time for you to be set free from this addiction; it took time for this addiction to wrap its arms around you, and it will take time to be set free from this worldly influence. Through God's grace, love, and the shedding of his blood is proof that you will be set free. Let us take a look at what God says about freedom.

To the Jews who had believed him, Jesus said, "If you hold to my teaching, you are really my disciples. Then you will know the truth, and the truth will set you free." They answered him, "We are Abraham's descendants and have never been slaves of anyone. How can you say that we shall be set **free**?" Jesus replied, "I tell you the truth, everyone who sins is a slave to sin. Now a slave has no permanent place in the family, but a son belongs to it forever. So if the Son sets you free, you will be free indeed. (John 8:31–36)

It is for **freedom** that Christ has set us **free**. Stand firm, then and do not let yourselves be burdened again by a yoke of slavery. (Galatians 5:1)

For we know that our old self was crucified with him so that the body of sin might be done away with, that we should no longer be slaves to sin because anyone who has died has been **freed** from sin. (Romans 6:6–7)

Therefore, there is now no condemnation for those who are in Christ Jesus, because through Christ Jesus the law of the Spirit of life set me **free** from the law of sin and death. (Romans 8:1–2)

For it is God's will that by doing good you should silence the ignorant talk of foolish men. Live as **free** men, but do not use your freedom as a cover-up for evil; live as servants of God. (1 Peter 2:15–16)

And from Jesus Christ, who is the faithful witness, the firstborn from the dead, and the ruler of the kings of the earth. To him who loves us and has **freed** us from our sins by his blood. (Revelation 1:5)

For all have sinned and fall short of the glory of God, and are justified **freely** by his **grace** through the redemption that came by Christ Jesus. (Romans 3:23–24)

Homework:

If you haven't done so already, make a list of those people you have hurt through this addiction and make a plan to ask for their forgiveness and try to reconcile with them. Remember, if they don't forgive you, give them over to God. This is part of the process of being set free.

More of my story: As stated in earlier in this journey, that night when Pastor Jim Garlow placed his hand on me and was talking with me about coming back to church and tackling me if I didn't return, that hand he had on my shoulder was tightening with every word he spoke to me. It felt like Spock from Star Trek had his Vulcan nerve pinch on me and I was going to pass out. Just kidding on the nerve pinch, but Pastor Jim did have a very firm grasp on my shoulder while he talked and prayed for me. While he was disappointed in me, he still cared for and loved me, just as Christ loves us no matter what. We just need to go to him and let him into our hearts and ask for forgiveness.

JOURNEY FIVE

Talk about last week's homework.

Statement of Truth:

Temptation is not a sin; acting on that temptation is.

Journey Five: Temptation

Every time I have fallen to the temptation (relapsed) of pornography, I have always come back to the same question—why? Why am I so weak? Why can't I have more self-control? Why can't I be stronger and beat this temptation thing? The key word here is "I"; there's no way that any of us can do this on our own or even think that we can beat this addiction all by ourselves. I believe that once we have the ability to fight off temptation, we will be more successful in breaking these chains that bind us from becoming closer to Jesus Christ.

Can you think of the very first act of weakness or lack of self-control, or the lack of an accountability partner in the Bible? If you guessed Adam and Eve in the garden of Eden, you are right. But what really happened in the garden of Eden? Let us travel back to the beginning, when temptation first entered into our life society.

When God formed man (Adam) from the dust of the earth (see Genesis 2:7), he put him in charge of the garden of Eden, where trees grew and rivers ran through the land. How perfect was that—to live in a garden that was so rich and beautiful and supplied all that we needed! Then the Lord said, "It is not good for the man to be alone. I will make a helper suitable for him" (Genesis 2:18). So the Lord God caused the man to fall into a deep sleep, and while he was sleeping, he took one of the man's ribs and closed up the place with flesh. Then the Lord God made a woman from the rib he had taken out of the man, and he brought her to the man. The man said, "This is now bone of my bones and flesh of my flesh; she shall be called 'woman,' for she was taken out of man" (Genesis 2:21–23).

If you think about it, this is our first accountability partner. This is Adam's wife; it was his responsibility to make sure she was taken care of, protected, and loved. What better way to be held accountable to his wife and to God as well. God gave Adam two gifts: the garden to take care of, and Eve, to be a suitable mate, allowing the two of them to become one with God.

Your wife, if you are married, should be your number-one accountability partner. Of course, the more accountability partners you have, the better off you are in fighting off temptation.

Now let's take a closer look at the first time man was tempted—the lack of self-control and the lack of accountability.

> Now the serpent was more crafty than any of the wild animals the Lord God had made. He said to the woman, "Did God really say, 'You must not eat from any tree in the garden'?" [the first sign of temptation]. The woman said to the serpent, "We may eat fruit from

the trees in the garden, but God did say, 'You must not eat fruit from the tree that is in the middle of the garden, and you must not touch it, or you will die.'" (Genesis 3:1–3)

Question: Did God directly tell Eve not to eat from the Tree of Life? Read Genesis 2:17 to find the answer.

"You will not surely die," the serpent said to the woman. "For God knows that when you eat of it your eyes will be opened, and you will be like God, knowing good and evil." When the woman saw that the fruit of the tree was good for food and **pleasing to the eye**, (what is pornography to us?) and also desirable for gaining wisdom, she took some and ate it. She also gave some to her husband, who was with her, and he at it. Then the eyes of both of them were opened, and they realized they were naked; so they sewed fig leaves together and made coverings for themselves. (Genesis 3:4–7)

We see here that the woman was tempted by Satan, which led to the woman giving in to that temptation (weakness) and eventually eating the fruit from the tree (self-control). But what happened to her accountability partner, Adam? Where was he? Was he with her? He, too, was weak and ate from the tree. Why did Adam fall to temptation? Satan was not talking to Adam; he was tempting Eve.

The answer: both Adam and Eve took their eyes off of God. God provided everything they needed, but they looked elsewhere for their needs instead of trusting in the Lord. This is what we do when we fail to keep our focus on the Lord and seek self-pleasure while addicted to pornography.

The big question is, what will it take for men to break these chains and get away from pornography in a world that views pornography as a freedom of expression while others say, "Well it's not hurting anyone, so why should we ban pornography or make it illegal?"

The answer to these questions is pretty simple; it's just hard for men to apply what God says about sexual immorality. Those of you who are Christian men going through this study know quite well what God's Word says about sex. We need to keep our focus on the Lord and not on our desires; we all know it's easier said than done, but that is why we need accountability partners and prayer. Prayer takes a key role in our healing process, but we will discuss that later in this study.

Notes:

_____

_____

_____

_____

_____

_____

_____

_____

_____

_____

_____

_____

What does God's Word say about temptation?

When **tempted**, no one should say, "God is tempting me," for God cannot be tempted by evil, nor does he **tempt** anyone; but each one is **tempted** when, by his own evil desire, he is dragged away and enticed. Then, after desire has conceived, it gives birth to sin, and sin, when it is full-grown, gives birth to death. Don't be deceived, my dear brothers. Every good and perfect gift is from above, coming down from the Father of the heavenly lights, who does not change like shifting shadows. He chose to give us birth through the Word of truth, that we might be kind of firstfruits of all he created. (James 1:13–18)

For we do not have a high priest who is unable to sympathize with our **weaknesses**, but we have one who has been **tempted** in every way, just as we are-yet was without sin. Let us then approach the throne of grace with confidence, **so that we may receive mercy and find grace to help us in our time of need.** (Hebrews 4:15–16)

For this reason he had to be made like his brothers in every way, in order that he might become a merciful and faithful high priest in service to God, and that he might make atonement for the sins of the people. **<u>Because he himself suffered when he was tempted, he is able to help those who are being tempted.</u>** (Hebrews 2:17–18)

This is another reason to be set free from pornography. Once you are free from this addiction, you will be an example to others who suffer from this addition and will help them to be free from their chains.

No temptation has seized you except what is common to man. And God is faithful; he will not let you be tempted beyond what you can bear. But when you are tempted, he will also provide a way out so that you can stand up under it. (1 Corinthians 10:13)

Homework:

Please read the following Scriptures:

1. Luke 4:1–13
2. Ephesians 6:10–20 (This is the Armor of God prayer, one of the best ways to fight off temptation; you should memorize the Armor of God prayer.)

ONE MAN'S TESTIMONY

In Sep. 23rd 2012, two months after I married my wife, I registered on a dating web site to solicit sex. I did it on a weekend she was on a trip with family. I also did it on a day I had my two children in my care. The only thing that mattered was to find a partner with the only purpose to share an outdoor exercise regimen have intimacy. I had only been about two weeks since my last intimate encounter with my wife because of our work schedule and other things that kept us occupied. In a short time I felt desperate for an outlet, so I registered and contacted a few ladies.

Two days later my wife found, I confessed, divulged and shared with her my profile account where she saw my interactions. Aside from impacting my wife my incident made her think that I've probably been with other women during the course of our relationship.

At this time I had flash backs of the many times I did things and had to look over my shoulder. The times I was being covert and sneaky. I finally took a good look in the mirror and saw that I think about sex very often, I've lied and exercise other habits that support these behaviors. Such as occasionally viewing porn, visiting strip clubs was condoned in this relationship and the last one. I would view and fantasize about women in social websites such as Facebook, Twitter, health magazines and in person. In my mind I created a world I was not able to live out during my 39 years of breathing life. About 15 years of molding myself in to a person that was at the brink of having an affair.

Thereafter I joined Unleashed Warriors (UW); it's a support group that helps men in the struggle against sexual addiction. Since I have learned to start processing the fact that in my family apparent addiction, I grew up in a very dysfunctional family where heavy corporal punishment was exercised. I was emotionally abused, my mom was never home and both my parents felt distant. At school I was often made fun of because of my Hispanic name referred to as "Joser". As I grew older I never learned to let go. I learned to be resentful, hatful, raged, selfish and vindictive. In my previous relationship I was very unfaithful and used sex as a way to cope with many unresolved issues.

Life Skills and U.W. program has taught me to start identifying critical issues in my healing process. I've learned to let go of a lot of resentment in my past. I've also learned to take better approach in other areas of my life. Slowly I have been breaking down my secret world that took me many years to create.

I'm grateful that I still have the love and full support of my wife.

My goal is to continue to work on improving my relationship with GOD, my wife and children, to also continue to identify any non-secure areas in my heart and mind. I feel my first step in change is recognition (being honest with God, myself & others) the second is taking initiative to move forward. Without that effort I can never know what it will be like to heal and bring transformation in my family. Without effort I cannot know the power of GODS grace and have victory over this addiction.

JOURNEY SIX

Statement of Truth:

Only through God can we be strong enough to fight off our sin.

<u>Journey Six:</u> Heaven or Hell

Here is a most important question for all of us: where would you like to go—heaven or hell? Personally I choose heaven; I want to be with our Lord and Savior and redeemer.

When we accidently cut ourselves and start bleeding, what do we do with the open cut? We clean the wound and place a Band-Aid on it to allow the wound to heal and to keep it protected from dirt and other foreign matters so it won't get infected, and if it's a deep wound, we apply pressure to stop the bleeding. We have a deep cut, and it's infected by the sin of pornography, and we can't afford to just put a Band-Aid on our infection; now is the time to apply pressure to stop the bleeding.

Each day that goes by and you don't relapse back to pornography is a victory for Jesus Christ! But staying in recovery all the time can be strenuous because of all the temptations that Satan and the world throws at us. How do we stay in recovery so we can defeat this addiction and finally be free from these chains? Again, the answers are indeed simple. We can stay in recovery through prayer, accountability, reading the Bible daily, memorizing Scripture, attending Christian counseling sessions and studies like this one, and becoming involved with your local Christian church. These are tools that we can use every time we feel the stress of temptation.

Let us take a look at heaven and hell, and then you can decide where you would like to spend the rest of your life. If you want to go to hell, then stay in this addiction; if you want to go to heaven with our Lord and Savior, then that, too, is your choice. Either way, you have a very important decision to make.

Following is some of what Scripture tells us about heaven.

> The Lord reigns, let nations tremble; he sits enthroned between the cherubim, let the earth shake. Great is the Lord in Zion; he is exalted over all the nations. (Psalm 99:1–2)

This tells us that our God is looking down upon us and sees everything.

> This is what the Lord says: "**Heaven is my throne**, and the earth is my footstool. Where is the house you will build for me? Where will my resting place be? Has not my hand made all these things, and so they came into being?" declares the Lord. (Isaiah 66:1–2)

> Behold, I will create new **heavens** and a new earth. The former things will not be remembered, nor will they come to mind. But be glad and rejoice forever in what I will create, for I will create Jerusalem to be a delight and its people a joy. (Isaiah 65:17–18)

"Do not store up for yourselves treasures on earth, where moth and rust destroy, and where thieves break in and steal. But store up for yourselves treasures in heaven, where moth and rust do not destroy, and where thieves do not break in and steal. For where your treasure is, there your heart will be also. (Matthew 6:19–21)

"When the Son of Man comes in his glory, and all the angels with him, he will sit on his throne in **heavenly** glory. (Matthew 25:31)

Not that I have already obtained all this, but I press on to take hold of that for which Christ Jesus took hold of me. Brothers, I do not consider myself yet to have taken hold of it. But one thing I do: Forgetting what is behind and straining toward what is ahead, I press on toward the goal to win the prize for which God has called me **heavenward** in Christ Jesus. (Philippians 3:12–14)

After this I looked, and there before me was a door standing open in heaven. And the voice I had first heard speaking to me like a trumpet said, "Come up here, and I will show you what must take place after this." At once I was in the Spirit, and there before me was a throne in heaven with some sitting on it. (Revelation 4:1–2)

Then I saw a new heaven and a new earth, for the first heaven and the first earth had passed away, and there was no longer any sea. I saw the Holy City, the new Jerusalem, coming down out of heaven from God, prepared as a bride beautifully dressed for her husband. And I heard a loud voice from the throne saying, "Now the dwelling of God is with men, and he will live with them. They will be his people, and God himself will be with them and be their God. He will wipe every tear from their eyes. There will be no more death or mourning or crying or pain, for the old order of things has passed away." (Revelation 21:1–4)

Now let us see what Scripture says about hell. Hell is a place of eternal punishment and sorrow, and evil men. They prey on the barren and childless woman, and they show no kindness to the widow. But God drags away the mighty by his power; though they become established, they have no assurance of life. He may let them rest in a feeling of security, but his eyes are on their ways. For a little while they are gone; they are brought low and gathered up like all others; they are cut off like heads of grain. "If this is not so, who can prove me false and reduce my words to nothing?" Job 24:21-26

For all can see that wise men die; the foolish and the senseless alike perish and leave their wealth to others. Their tombs will remain their houses forever, their dwellings for endless generations, though they had named lands after themselves. But man, despite his riches, does not endure; he is like the beasts that perish. This is the fate of those who trust in themselves, and of their followers, who approve their sayings. Like sheep they are destined for the grave, and death will feed on them. The upright will rule over them in the morning; their forms will decay in the grave, far from their princely mansions. But God will redeem my life from the grave; he will surely take me to himself. (Psalm 49:10–15)

Multitudes who sleep in the dust of the earth will awake: some to everlasting life, others to shame and everlasting contempt. (Daniel 12:2)

Those who live according to the sinful nature have their minds set on what that nature desires; but those who live in accordance with the Spirit have their minds set on what the Spirit desires. The mind of sinful man is death, but the mind controlled by the Spirit is life and peace; the sinful mind is hostile to God. It does not submit to God's law, nor can it do so. Those controlled by the sinful nature cannot please God. (Romans 8:5–7)

He will punish those who do not know God and do not obey the gospel of our Lord Jesus. They will be punished with everlasting destruction and shut out from the presence of the Lord and from the majesty of his power on the day he comes to be glorified in his holy people and to be marveled at among all those who believed. (2 Thessalonians 1:8–10)

Then death and Hades were thrown into the lake of fire. The lake of fire is the second death. If anyone's name was not found written in the book of life, he was thrown into the lake of fire. (Revelation 20:14–15)

So what is it going to take for you to stay in recovery and keep out of relapse? Will you choose heaven or hell? If you don't fight to be free from pornography, you will lose your marriage, your family, your job, and your soul! Let's take a look at one more piece of Scripture that tells God's love for us and also tells us what happens if we do evil.

"For God so love the world that he gave his one and only Son, that whoever believes in him shall not perish but have eternal life. For God did not send his Son into the world to condemn the world, but to save the world through him. Whoever believes in him is not condemned, but whoever does not believe stands condemned already because he has not believed in the name of God's one and only Son. <u>This is the verdict: Light has come into the world, but men loved darkness instead of light because their deeds were evil. Everyone who does evil hates the light, and will not come into the light for fear that his deeds will be exposed.</u> But whoever lives by the truth comes into the light, so that it may be seen plainly that what he has done has been done through God. (John 3:16–21)

Homework:

Write down a plan that will enable you to stay in recovery, even if it means changing your whole regular daily and weekly routine.

Notes:

_____

_____

_____

_____

_____

_____

_____

JOURNEY SEVEN

Statement of Truth:

You must rise up and fight against temptation, but let God fight and win the battles.

Journey Seven: The Armor of God

Let us first take a look at battles. How does God want us to handle our battles?

> He said: "Listen, King Jehoshaphat and all who live in Judah and Jerusalem! This is what the Lord says to you: 'Do not be afraid or discouraged because of this vast army. For the battle is not yours, but God's. Tomorrow march down against them. They will be climbing up by the Pass of Ziz, and you will find them at the end of the gorge in the Desert of Jeruel. <u>You will not have to fight this battle</u>. Take up your positions; stand firm and see the deliverance the Lord will give you, O Judah and Jerusalem. Do not be afraid; do not

be discouraged. Go out to face them tomorrow, and the Lord will be with you.'" (2 Chronicles 20:15–17)

Who is this King of glory? The Lord strong and mighty, the Lord mighty in battle. (Psalm 24:8)

The Lord will fight for you; you need only to be still." (Exodus 14:14)

The Lord your God, who is going before you, will fight for you, as he did for you in Egypt, before your very eyes, and in the desert. (Deuteronomy 1:30)

Do not be afraid of them; the Lord your God himself will fight for you." (Deuteronomy 3:22)

Wherever you hear the sound of the trumpet, join us there. Our God will fight for us!" (Nehemiah 4:20)

Contend, O Lord, with those who contend with me; fight against those who fight against me. Take up shield and buckler; arise and come to my aid. Brandish spear and javelin against those who pursue me. Say to my soul, "I am your salvation." (Psalm 35:1–3)

Jesus said, "My kingdom is not of this world. If it were, my servants would fight to prevent my arrest by the Jews. But now my kingdom is from another place." (John 18:36)

Timothy, my son, I give you this instruction in keeping with the prophecies once made about you, so that by following them you may fight the good fight, holding on to faith and a good conscience. Some have rejected these and so have shipwrecked their faith. (1 Timothy 1:18–19)

Fight the good fight of the faith. Take hold of the eternal life to which you were called when you made your good confession in the presence of many witnesses. (1 Timothy 6:12)

I have fought the good fight, I have finished the race, I have kept the faith. Now there is in store for me the crown of righteousness, which the Lord, the righteous Judge, will award to me on that day-and not only to me, but also to all who have longed for his appearing. (2 Timothy 4:7–8)

Explain what the above Scriptures mean to you.

Notes:

_____

_____

_____

_____

_____

_____

_____

_____

_____

_____

Throughout this whole study, I have been pushing you to know the armor of God and use this as the start of each day, and to help you fight off temptation. Let's take a more detailed look at the armor of God.

There are six pieces of armor that we need to dress in: the belt of truth, the breastplate of righteousness, the gospel of peace, the shield of faith, the helmet of salvation, and the sword of the spirit. But what do they really mean?

The Belt of Truth:

> Righteousness will be his belt and faithfulness the sash around his waist. (Isaiah 11:5)

> Yet a time is coming and has now come when the true worshipers will worship the Father in spirit and <u>truth</u>, for they are the kind of worshipers the Father seeks. God is spirit, and his worshipers <u>must worship in spirit and in truth</u>. (John 4:23–24)

> He who speaks on his own does so to gain honor for himself, but he who works for the honor of the one who sent him is a man of truth; there is nothing false about him. (John 7:18)

We know that Satan is the father of all lies. His primary weapon is deception. But using the truth is our first line of defense and the first step in any recovery program. John 8:32 is one of the most popular Scriptures regarding truth. Then you will know the truth, and *the truth will set you free.* You can't get any clearer than that regarding being set free from pornography!

Jesus answered, "<u>I am the way and the truth and the life</u>. No one comes to the Father except through me." (John 14:6)

The belt seems to hold the rest of the armor together; it's like the centerpiece of our clothing that holds firm against our bodies. Let's take a look at one more part of Scripture pertaining to truth. "Grace, mercy, and peace from God the Father and from Jesus Christ, the Father's Son, <u>will be with us in truth and love</u>" (2 John 1:3).

The Breastplate of Righteousness:

"Fashion a breastpiece for making decisions-the work of a skilled craftsman" (Exodus 28:15). This is the first sign of a breastplate in the Bible.

"He put on righteousness as his **breastplate**, and the helmet of salvation on his head; he put on the garments of vengeance and wrapped himself in zeal as in a cloak" (Isaiah 59:17). Here we see more parts of the armor coming together for protection in a spiritual battle.

> But since we belong to the day, let us be self-controlled, putting on faith and love as a breastplate, and the hope of salvation as a helmet. (1 Thessalonians 5:8)

> Each day we need to have victory over our eternal destiny and to do that we must have confession of our sins which will clear the way for righteousness in our daily struggles. <u>But seek first his kingdom and his righteousness, and all these things will be given to you as well. Therefore do not worry about tomorrow, for tomorrow will worry about itself. Each day has enough trouble of its own.</u> (Matthew 6:33–34)

Let the Lord judge the peoples. Judge me, O Lord, according to my righteousness, according to my integrity, O Most High. O righteous God, who searches minds and hearts, bring to an end the violence of the wicked and make the righteous secure. (Psalm 7:8–9)

"Blessed are they whose transgressions are forgiven, whose sins are covered. Blessed is the man whose sin the Lord will never count against him." Romans 4:7–8. For through the law I died to the law so that I might live for God. I have been crucified with Christ and I no longer live, but Christ lives in me. The life I live in the body, I live by faith in the Son of God, who loved me and gave himself for me. I do not set aside the grace of God, for if righteousness could be gained through the law, Christ died for nothing!" (Galatians 2:19–21)

He himself bore our sins in his body on the tree, so that we might die to sins and live for righteousness; by his wounds you have been healed. For you were like sheep going astray, but now you have returned to the Shepherd and Overseer of your souls. (1 Peter 2:2)

The Gospel of Peace:

Knowing that we can take refuge in God gives us a since of peace towards our addiction. "And with your feet fitted with the readiness that comes from the Gospel of peace." Ephesians 6:15.

Come, my children, listen to me; I will teach you the fear of the Lord. Whoever of you loves life and desires to see many good days, keep your tongue from evil and your lips from speaking lies. Turn from evil and do good; <u>seek peace and pursue it.</u> (Psalm 34:11–14)

<u>Let the peace of Christ rule in your hearts</u>, since as members of one body you were called to peace. And be thankful. (Colossians 3:15)

Finally, all of you, live in harmony with one another; be sympathetic, love as brothers, be compassionate and humble. Do not repay evil with evil or insult with insult, but with blessing, because to this you were called so that you may inherit a blessing. For, "Whoever would love life and see good days must keep his tongue from evil and his lips from deceitful speech. He must turn from evil and do good; <u>he must seek peace and pursue it</u>. (1 Peter 3:8–11)

<u>For he himself is our peace</u>, who has made the two one and has destroyed the barrier, the dividing wall of hostility, by abolishing in his flesh the law with its commandments and regulations. His purpose was to create in himself one new man out of two, thus making peace, and in this one body to reconcile both of them to God through the cross, by which he put to death their hostility. He came and preached peace to you who were far away and peace to those who were near. (Ephesians 2:14–17)

Be completely humble and gentle; be patient, bearing with one another in love. Make every effort to keep unity of the Spirit through the <u>bond of peace</u>. (Ephesians 4:2–3)

We are to be peacemakers and bring people together in Christ name. Let us therefore make every effort to do what leads to peace and to mutual edification. (Romans 14:19)

The Shield of Faith:

In battle, the shield is known for protection against spears, arrows, and the waling of swords. Let us see what God's Word says about his shield.

The Lord is my strength and <u>my shield</u>; my heart trusts in him, and I am helped. My heart leaps for joy and I will give thanks to him in song. (Psalm 28:7)

<u>My shield</u> is God Most High, who saves the upright in heart. Psalm 7:10.

Consequently, **faith** comes from hearing the message, and the message is heard through the word of Christ. (Romans 10:17)

This righteousness from God comes through **faith** in Jesus Christ to all who believe. There is no difference, for all have sinned and fall short of the glory of God, and are justified freely by his grace through the redemption that came by Christ Jesus. (Romans 3:22–24)

> For it is by grace you have been saved, through **faith**-and this not from yourselves, it is the gift of God-not by works, so that no one can boast. (Ephesians 2:8–9)

> You foolish man, do you want evidence that **faith** without deeds is useless? Was not our ancestor Abraham considered righteous for what he did when he offered his son Isaac on the altar? You see that is **faith** and his actions were working together, and his **faith** was made complete by what he did. (James 2:20–22)

Whenever you feel tempted or have a deceptive thought or accusation, meet it head-on with God's Word. How did Jesus protect himself from the temptations that Satan was throwing at him? By the knowledge of God's words.

The Helmet of Salvation:

At the time of the writing of this study, "my son. Apollo is in the US army and is in Afghanistan. He wears a helmet that is part of his daily uniform while out on patrol."

These helmets are made to withstand a mighty blow from either a gunshot or flying shrapnel. How does the helmet of salvation protect us?

> He put on righteousness as his breastplate, and the **helmet** of salvation on his head. (Isaiah 59:17)

> But since we belong to the day, let us be self-controlled, putting on faith and love as a breastplate, and the hope of **salvation as a helmet**. For God did not appoint us to suffer wrath but to receive **salvation** through our Lord Jesus Christ. (1 Thessalonians 5:8–9)

As we go about our daily routines, we struggle with what the Devil throws at us and our flesh, but our salvation is based on Christ's good works, not our own good works.

> That if you confess with your mouth, Jesus is Lord," and believe in your heart that God raised him from the dead, you will be **saved**. For it is with your heart that you believe and are justified, and it is with your mouth that you confess and are saved. (Romans 10:9–10)

> Jesus said to him, "Today salvation has come to this house, because this man, too, is a son of Abraham. For the Son of Man came to seek and to **save** what was lost." (Luke 19:9–10)

> Since we have now been justified by his blood, how much more shall we be **saved** from God's wrath through him! For if, when we were God's enemies, we were reconciled to him through the death of his Son, how much more, having been reconciled, shall we be **saved** through his life! (Romans 5:9–10)

> But because of his great love for us, God, who is rich in mercy, made us alive with Christ even when we were dead in transgressions-it is by grace you have been **saved**. (Ephesians 2:4–5)

We must wear this Helmet of Salvation to ward off the temptation of doubting our salvation. But God's Word says,

> For he has rescued us from the dominion of darkness and brought us into the kingdom of the Son he loves,

in whom we have redemption, the forgiveness of sins. (Colossians 1:13–14)

The Sword of the Spirit:

The first five parts of this spiritual body armor are considered defensive armor that protects us from the Devil's schemes and against the powers of this dark world and against the spiritual forces of evil in the heavenly realms. The sword is the only offensive weapon. Let us take a closer look at this double-edged sword.

> God is a righteous judge, a God who expresses his wrath every day. If he does not relent, he will sharpen his **sword**; he will bend and string his bow. (Psalm 7:11–12)

> For the word of God is living and active. Sharper than any **double-edged sword**, it penetrates even to dividing soul and spirit, joints and marrow; it judges the thoughts and attitudes of the heart. (Hebrews 4:12)

> For he is God's servant to do you good. But if you do wrong, be afraid, for he does not bear the **sword** for nothing. He is God's servant, an agent of wrath to bring punishment on the wrongdoer. (Romans 13:4)

> So that the thoughts of many hearts will be revealed. And a **sword** will pierce your own soul too. (Luke 2:35)

In Matthew 10:32–36, Jesus says, "Do not suppose that I have come to bring peace to the earth. I did not come to bring peace, but a **sword**. For I have come to turn "'a man against his father, a daughter against her mother, a daughter-in-law against her mother-in-law, a man's enemies will be the members of his own household.'"" What does this passage mean to you?

"Reckless words pierce like a **sword**, but the tongue of the wise brings healing" (Proverbs 12:18). So the **tongue** can be mightier than a sword? What do you think?

We all know about when the Devil led Jesus by the spirit into the desert to be tempted in Matthew 4:1–11. So what happened? Jesus spoke the words of the Lord, and the Devil left him, and angels came and attended him.

So I tell you, be knowledgeable in God's Word, read the Bible each day, and spend time with our Lord so you, too, can fight off the Devil's schemes.

Homework:

Read 2 Corinthians 10:3–7.

Write a paragraph explaining where you are in your journey to becoming free from this addiction. You must be completely honest. Be prepared to read your statement.

JOURNEY EIGHT

Statement of Truth:

Humbleness leads to God's Grace.

Journey Eight: Grace

"He has showed you, O man, what is good. And what does the Lord require of you? To act justly and to love mercy and to walk humbly with your God" (Micah 6:8). God's grace for us is so wonderful that we are not good enough to look upon him. We will never measure up to Jesus Christ, but we can be humble enough to receive God's grace. Let's see what the Scripture says about God's grace.

Let us read Luke 15:11–31 and discuss how this parable relates to you.

Notes:

_____

_____

_____

_____

Therefore, since we have been justified through **faith**, we have **peace** with God through our Lord Jesus Christ, through whom we have gained access by faith into this **grace** in which we now stand. And we rejoice in the hope of the glory of God. Not only so, but we also rejoice in our sufferings, because we know that suffering produces perseverance; perseverance, character; and character, hope. And hope does not disappoint us, because God has poured out his love into our hearts by the Holy Spirit, whom he has given us. (Romans 5:1–5)

Nevertheless, death reigned from the time of Adam to the time of Moses, even over those who did not sin by breaking a command, as did Adam, who was a pattern of the one to come. But the gift is not like the trespass. For if the many died by the trespass of the one man, how much more did God's **grace** and the gift that came by the **grace** of one man, Jesus Christ, overflow to the many! (Romans 5:14–15)

For just as through the disobedience of the one man the many were made sinners, so also through the obedience of the one man the many will be made righteous. The law was added so that the trespass might increase. But where sin increased, **grace** increased all the more, so that, just as sin reigned in death, so also **grace** might reign through righteousness to bring eternal life through Jesus Christ our Lord. (Romans 5:19–21)

God loves us despite our sinful nature.

As for you, you were dead in your transgressions and sins, in which you used to live when you followed the ways of this world and of the ruler of the kingdom of the air, the spirit who is now at work in those who are disobedient. All of us also lived among them at one time, gratifying the cravings of our sinful nature and following its desires and thoughts. Like the rest, we were by nature objects of wrath. But because of his great love for us, God, who is rich in mercy, made us alive with Christ even when we were dead in transgressions—it is by grace you have been saved. (Ephesians 2:1–5)

If we are to receive grace from God, we must be humble in our sins.

At that time the disciples came to Jesus and asked, "Who is the greatest in the kingdom of heaven?" He called a little child and had him stand among them. And he said: "I tell you the truth, unless you change and become like little children, you will never enter the kingdom of heaven. Therefore, whoever **humbles** himself like this child is the greatest in the kingdom of heaven. (Matthew 18:1–4)

We must also get rid of our pride and put no confidence in our flesh, for if we become humble, then humility is confidence properly placed in God.

> For it is we who are the circumcision, we who worship by the Spirit of God, who glory in Christ Jesus, and who put no confidence in the flesh—though I myself have reasons for such confidence. (Philippians 3:3–4)

> Do nothing out of selfish ambition or vain conceit, but in **humility** consider others better than yourselves. Each of you should look not only to your own interests, but also to the interests of others. Your attitude should be the same as that of Christ Jesus. (Philippians 2:4–5)

Young men, in the same way be submissive to those who are older. All of you, clothe yourselves with <u>humility</u> toward one another, because, "God opposes the proud but gives grace to the <u>humble</u>." <u>Humble</u> yourselves, therefore, under God's mighty hand, that he may lift you up in due time. Cast all your anxiety on him because he cares for you. (1 Peter 4:5–6)

Let us then approach the throne of **grace** with confidence, so that we may receive mercy and find grace to help us in our time of need. Hebrews 4:16.

As God's fellow workers we urge you not to receive God's **grace** in vain. For he says, "In the time of my favor I heard you, and in the day of salvation I helped you." I tell you, now is the time of God's favor, now is the day of salvation. (2 Corinthians 6:22)

For you know the grace of our Lord Jesus Christ, that though he was rich, yet for your sakes he became poor, so that you through his poverty might become rich. (2 Corinthians 8:9)

And God is able to make all grace abound to you, so that in all things at all times, having all that you need you will abound in every good work. As it is written: "He has scattered abroad his gifts to the poor; his righteousness endures forever." (2 Corinthians 9:8)

But he gives us more grace. That is why Scripture says, "God opposes the proud but gives <u>grace to the Humble</u>" (James 4:6).

Can you relate to the following list of pride?

- I think of myself more highly than others.
- I think of myself as better than others because of my accomplishments.
- I think of myself as more spiritual and devoted than others.
- I think my needs should come before the needs of others.
- I think of gaining recognition by attaining titles or positions.
- I think about getting the credit I feel I deserve.
- I think I find it hard to admit when I am wrong.
- I think I am more concerned about pleasing people than pleasing God.
- I think I have a stronger desire to do my will than God's will.
- I think I lean on my own understanding rather than God's understanding.
- I think I am more concerned about controlling others than controlling myself.
- I think I have no needs at all.
- I think I rely on my own strengths and knowledge instead of the power of the Holy Spirit.
- I think I am too busy doing my important things to take the time to do things for others.
- I think I can handle and control my own addiction.
- I don't need any help from anyone; my addiction isn't that bad.
- I have been watching porn for years, and it hasn't hurt anyone.
- I turned out just fine; I am not a rapist, murder, adulterer, or a thief.
- I admit I am addicted to porn; I am not in denial.
- I am a Christian, and God will always forgive me.
- I have no use for an accountability partner.

Homework:

Make your own list of the top ten prides, rating them on a scale of 1–10, one being the worst pride and ten the least. Bring your list to class for discussion.

ONE MAN'S TESTIMONY

My story was about denial. I did not see what was wrong about lusting and masturbation. Didn't all men do that? After all, my sex life with my wife was non-existent. That's how I justified my behavior. After becoming a Christian I realized that I was committing adultery without having an affair. God's word is very clear about that. I knew I had to do something. Trying to do something on my own power never worked. I included God, with the same results. It wasn't until I joined up with a group of men (Unleashed Warriors) through my church who all struggled with similar addictions that my life began to change. The group provided a safe environment, where you were not judged. Jesus is the centerpiece, where hope abounds. With the support of other men keeping you accountable and the grace the Lord provides I am able to see myself moving towards the healing my flesh longs for; a healing over this sexual addiction.

JOURNEY NINE

Statement of Truth:

May I never boast except in the cross of our Lord Jesus Christ, through which the world has been crucified to **m**e, and I to the world. Galatians 6:14.

Journey Nine: The *M* in M*A*P

All of us know that the letter *M* stands for Men; let's take another look at some words that are related to pornography that start with the letter *M*.

Masturbation: Some say that masturbation is not a sin, what do you think? Let's look at Proverbs 5:21–23. We find there that a man's ways are in full view of the Lord, who examines all his paths. The evil deeds of a wicked man ensnare him; the cords of his sin hold him fast. He will die for lack of discipline, led astray by his own great folly.

When men masturbate, they are imagining or looking at images that help in this act of sexual immorality. This is still considered sex outside of marriage. With that said, masturbation is a sin.

But since there is so much immorality, each man should have his own wife and each woman her own husband. The husband should fill his marital duty to his wife, and likewise the wife to her husband. (1 Corinthians 7:2–3)

Do not deprive each other except by mutual consent and for a time, so that you may devote yourselves to prayer. (1 Corinthians 7:5)

You have heard that it was said, 'Do not commit adultery.' But I tell you that anyone who looks at a woman lustfully has already committed adultery with her in his heart. (Matthew 5:27–28)

It doesn't get any clearer than this.

<u>Me</u>: It's all about me! Like we have not heard this one before. Is it all about me? When we are caught up in our addiction, it seems like it is about "me." We have a tendency to manipulate life around us to make it seem like it's not about us. We try so hard to hide our sin that we actually live a life of denial and isolation. It's like a tennis match; we go back and forth, we serve our sinful addiction, and then we go forth to hide it from others.

Jesus turned and said to Peter, "Get behind me, Satan! You are a stumbling block to me; you do not have in mind the things of God, but the things of men. "Matthew 16:23.

An unfriendly man pursues selfish ends; he defies all sound judgment. A fool finds no pleasure in understanding but delights in airing his own opinions. Proverbs 18:1–2.

A man's own folly ruins his life, yet his heart rages against the Lord. Proverbs 19:3.

From the beginning, man was not meant to be a loner.

> The Lord God said, "It is not good for the man to be alone. I will make a helper suitable for him." (Genesis 2:18)

> For this reason a man will leave his father and mother and be united to his wife, and they will become one flesh. (Genesis 2:24)

You see, it's not all about me, it's about God! We are not alone, and our addiction does affect others.

<u>Money:</u> Billions of dollars a year are spent on the pornography business. How much have you spent on pornography? Do you find yourself working extra hours to earn more money to spend on this addiction? Have you ever not paid a bill because you wanted to buy pornographic products? What does the Bible say about money?

> No one can serve two masters. Either he will hate the one and love the other. Or he will be devoted to the one and despise the other. You cannot serve both God and Money. (Matthew 6:24)

> Do not store up for yourselves treasures on earth, where moth and rust destroy, and where thieves break in and steal. But store up for yourselves treasures in heaven, where moth and rust do not destroy, and where thieves do not break in and steal. For where your treasure is, there your heart will be also. (Matthew 6:19–20)

People who want to get rich fall into temptation and a trap and into many foolish and harmful desires that plunge men into ruin and destruction. For the love of money is a root of all kinds of evil. Some people, eager for money, have wandered from the faith and pierced themselves with many griefs. (1 Timothy 6:9–10

Here are other *M* words associated with pornography for discussion:

motive	mad	mentor
mood Swings	manipulate	maturing
mask	malnourished	mutual Love
mental	manifestation	marriage

Notes:

_____

_____

_____

_____

_____

_____

_____

_____

_____

_____

_____

_____

_____

_____

Men, what path does God have for you? I do believe it's not Satan's path to pornography! Once you realize in your heart that Jesus Christ bled to death on the cross for our sins, you will be set free from this addiction.

> They stripped him and put a scarlet robe on him, and then twisted together a crown of thorns and set it on his head. They put a staff in his right hand and knelt in front of him and mocked him. "Hail, King of the Jews!" they said. (Matthew 27:28–29)

> But the things that come out of the mouth come from the heart, and these make a man 'unclean.' For out of the heart come evil thoughts, murder, adultery, sexual immorality, theft, false testimony, slander. These are what make a man 'unclean'; but eating with unwashed hands does not make him 'unclean.'" (Matthew 15:18–20)

> Teach me your way, O Lord; lead me in a straight path because of my oppressors. (Psalm 27:11)

Homework:

Please read the following Scriptures:

1. Psalm 23:1–6 (The Shepherd's Psalm)
2. Proverbs 15:19
3. Proverbs 15:24
4. Proverbs 3:5–7

Remember to start and finish each day with the Armor of God prayer, Ephesians 6:10–19.

JOURNEY TEN

Discuss last week's homework.

Statement of Truth:

"What, then shall we say in response to this? If God is for us, who can be **against** us?" (Romans 8:31).

Journey Ten: The *A* in M*A*P

As we looked at the letter *M* in chapter ten, let us look at the letter *A*.

Anxiety: What does "anxiety" mean? It's a displeasing feeling of fear and concern that can create feelings of fear, worry, uneasiness, and dread. When anxiety becomes excessive, it may fall under the classification of an anxiety disorder. Another view defines anxiety as a future-oriented mood state in which one is ready to attempt to cope with upcoming negative events. So what does God say about anxiety?

> Then Jesus said to his disciples: "Therefore I tell you, do
> not worry about your life, what you will eat; or about

your body, what you will wear. Life is more than food, and the body more than clothes. (Luke 12:22–23)

Who of you by worrying can add a single hour to his life? Since you cannot do this very little thing, why do you worry about the rest? (Luke 12:25–26)

Do not be afraid, little flock, for your Father has been pleased to give you the kingdom. (Luke 12:32)

Do not be anxious about anything, but in everything, by prayer and petition, with thanksgiving, present your request to God. (Philippians 4:6)

Humble yourselves, therefore, under God's mighty hand, that he may lift you up in due time. Cast all you anxiety on him because he cares for you. (1 Peter 5:6–7)

An anxious heart weighs a man down, but a kind word cheers him up. (Proverbs 12:25)

How much anxiety do you have in your heart because of pornography?

Adultery is sexual infidelity to one's spouse. Even in cases of separation from one's spouse, an extramarital affair is still considered adultery.

Let us see what the Bible says about adultery.

The Lord said to Moses, Say to the Israelites: 'When a man or woman wrongs another in any way and so is unfaithful to the Lord, that person is guilty and must confess the sin he has committed. (Numbers 4:5–7)

When Uriah's wife heard that her husband was dead, she mourned for him. After the time of mourning was over, David had her brought to his house, and she became his wife and bore him a son. But the thing David had done displeased the Lord. (2 Samuel 11:26–27)

(Read 2 Samuel 11:1–27; this depicts the entire chapter, which details the sin of adultery).

Can a man scoop fire into his lap without his clothes being burned? Can a man walk on hot coals without his feet being scorched? So is he who sleeps with another man's wife; no one who touches her will go unpunished. (Proverbs 6:27–29)

But a man who commits adultery lacks judgment; whoever does so destroys himself. (Proverbs 6:32)

You have heard that it was said, 'Do not commit adultery.' But I tell you that anyone who looks at a woman lustfully has already committed adultery with her in his heart. (Matthew 5:27–28)

As stated in chapter ten, the above Scripture is an example for both masturbation and adultery.

You say, "Food for the stomach and stomach for food" –but God will destroy them both. The body is not meant for sexual immorality, but for the Lord, and the Lord for the body. (1 Corithians 6:13)

Flee from sexual immorality. All other sins a man commits are outside his body, but he who sins sexually

sins against his own body. Do you not know that your
body is a temple of the Holy Spirit, who is in you, whom
you have received from God? (1 Corinthians 6:18–19)

Who of us have committed or continue to commit adultery with
our hearts, mind, and bodies?

<u>Anger:</u> *Dispositional* anger is related more to character traits than
to instincts or cognitions. Irritability, sullenness, and churlishness are
examples of this anger.

Irritability is a form of anger that we most associate with pornography;
especially when we get angry at ourselves when we relapse back to our
addiction or when we get caught in our addiction.

Let's see what Scripture says about anger.

Now the people complained about their hardships in
the hearing of the Lord, and when he heard them his
anger was aroused. Then fire from the Lord burned
among them and consumed some of the outskirts of the
camp. When the people cried out to Moses, he prayed to
the Lord and the fire died down. (Numbers 11:1–2)

Therefore each of you must put off falsehood and speak
truthfully to his neighbor, for we are all members of one
body. "In your **anger** do not sin": Do not let the sun
go down while you are still **angry**, and do not give the
devil a foothold. (Ephesians 4:25–27)

Get rid of all bitterness, rage and anger, brawling and
slander, along with every form of malice. Be kind and
compassionate to one another, forgiving each other, just
as in Christ God forgave you. (Ephesians 4:31–32)

My dear brothers, take note of this: Everyone should be quick to listen, slow to speak and slow to become **angry**, for man's anger does not bring about the righteous life that God desires. (James 1:19–20)

How many times have you taken your anger out on your spouse, friends, coworkers, and others because you are angry at yourself for being addicted to porn?

Here are other *A* words associated with pornography for discussion:

addicted	act	aggressive
actions	ability	ambitions
angered	accessing	accountability
adulteress	appetite	admire
attitudes	attractive	admitting

Notes:

_____

_____

_____

_____

_____

_____

_____

_____

_____

_____

We should not live our lives against God, but each time you view pornography, you are sinning against our Lord. Our goal is to be free from this addiction, and with the grace of God, you will be freed. You should also remember that the Son of Man has authority on earth. "But so that you may know that the Son of Man has authority on earth to forgive sins" (Matthew 9:6).

Homework:

Please read the following Scriptures:

1. Titus 3:1–2
2. Romans 13:1–2
3. 1 Peter 3:22
4. 1 Corinthians 10:8
5. Matthew 28:18

Pray the Armor of God prayer, Ephesians 6:10–20, each morning and each night.

JOURNEY ELEVEN

Discuss last week's homework.

Statement of Truth:

Sought through prayer and meditation to improve our conscious contact with God, praying only for knowledge of God's will for us and the power to carry that out.

Journey Eleven: The *P* in M*A*P

Just as we focused on the letters *M* and *A* in chapters ten and eleven, we will focus on the letter *P* in this chapter.

Purity:

It is God's will that you should be sanctified: that each of you should learn to control his own body in a way that is holy and honorable. Not in passionate lust like the heathen, who do not know God; and that in this matter no one should wrong his brother or take advantage of

> him. The Lord will punish men for all such sins, as we
> have already told you and warned you. For God did not
> call us to be impure, but to live a holy life. Therefore, he
> who rejects this instruction does not reject man but God,
> who gives his Holy Spirit. (1 Thessalonians 4:3–8).

It's God's will for us to be pure, and he gives us the power to carry that out, but we make the choice to sin and be impure in our addiction. Now is the time for you to choose to stay pure and rid yourself of pornography.

Pride:

> To fear the Lord is to hate evil; I hate pride and arrogance,
> evil behavior and perverse speech. (Proverbs 8:13)

> He who loves pleasure will become poor; whoever loves
> wine and oil will never be rich. (Proverbs 21:17)

> The eyes of the arrogant man will be humbled and the
> pride of men brought low; the Lord alone will be exalted
> in that day. (Isaiah 2:11)

Or do you think Scripture says without reason that the spirit he caused to live in us envies intensely? But he gives us more grace. That is why Scripture says, "God opposes the proud but gives grace to the humble" (James 4:5–6). Young men, in the same way be submissive to those who are older. All of you, clothe yourselves with humility toward one another, because "God opposes the proud but gives grace to the humble."

> Humble yourselves, therefore, under God's mighty
> hand, that he may lift you up in due time. Cast all

your anxiety on him because he cares for you. (1 Peter 5:5–7).

Are you ready to be fully humbled by the grace of God and be cleansed from pornography?

PRAYER:

A prayer to be rescued from the enemy:

> O Lord, you have seen this; be not silent.
> Do not be far from me, O Lord. Awake,
> And rise to my defense! Contend for me,
> my God and Lord. Vindicate me in your
> righteousness, O Lord my God; do not let
> them gloat over me. (Psalm 35:22–24)

Prayer is something we should start each day with; as I have been stressing throughout this study, start your day with the Armor of God prayer.

One of the most well-known prayers can be prayed toward our addiction to porn.

> Our Father in heaven,
> hallowed be your name,
> your kingdom come,
> your will be done
> On earth as it is in heaven.
> Give us today our daily bread.
> Forgive us our debts,
> as we also have forgiven our debtors.
> And lead us not into **temptation**,
> but deliver us from the evil one. (Matthew 6:9–13)

> Watch and pray so that you will not fall into **temptation**. The spirit is willing, but the body is weak. (Matthew 26:41).

> I pray that out of his glorious riches he may strengthen you with power through his spirit in your inner being, so that Christ may dwell in your hearts through faith. (Ephesians 3:16–17)

> But he said to me, "My grace is sufficient for you, for my power is made perfect in weakness." Therefore I will boast all the more gladly about my weaknesses, so that Christ's power may rest on me. That is why, for Christ's sake, I delight in weaknesses, in insults, in hardships, in persecutions, in difficulties. For when I am weak, then I am strong. (2 Corinthians 12:9–10)

Ask God to give you wisdom to help you in times of temptation. As stated in James 1:5–7, if any of you lacks wisdom, he should ask God, who gives generously to all without finding fault, and it will be given to him.

There must be daily prayer in your life so God can fight to break the chains that bind you to pornography, or you will never be able to be set free. Are you ready to be set free? Read James 5:13–17 to learn of the healing power of prayer.

Let us take a look at some other words related to porn that also start with the letter *P*.

Peace	Persecution	Power
Pain	Patience	Praise
Pleasure	Prison	Profanity
Punishment	Prostitution	Provoked
Practice	Poison	Powerless

Notes:

_____

_____

_____

_____

_____

_____

_____

_____

Prayer is the most important gift that God has blessed us with to stay in constant contact with him and have a close relationship with our spiritual Father.

> In the same way, the Spirit helps us in our weakness. We do not know what we ought to pray for, but the Spirit himself **intercedes** for us with groans that words cannot express. And he who searches our hearts knows the mind of the Spirit, because the Spirit **intercedes** for the saints in accordance with God's will. (Romans 8:26–27)

> But because Jesus lives forever, he has a permanent priesthood. Therefore he is able to save completely those who come to God through him, because he always lives to **intercede** for them. (Hebrews 7:24–25)

> I want men everywhere to lift up holy hands in prayer, without anger or disputing. (1 Timothy 2:8)

Read the entire verse of 1 Timothy 2:1–8.

Homework:

If you haven't already done so through this study, read Ephesians 6:10–17 and memorize this verse; I promise it does help fight against our addiction. Each week, stay in touch with your accountability partner.

And read Psalm 51, the Confession and Prayer for God's Pardon.

Before we conclude this study, let's sing "Amazing Grace (My Chains Are Gone)."

<u>Amazing Grace</u>

Amazing grace how sweet the sound that saved a wretch like me
I once was lost, but now I'm found was blind, but now I see
'Twas grace that taught my heart to fear and grace my fears relieved
How precious did that grace appear the hour I first believed
My chains are gone, I've been set free my God, my Savior has
ransomed me
And like a flood His mercy reigns Unending love, amazing grace
The Lord has promised good to me His word my hope secures
He will my shield and portion be as long as life endures
My chains are gone, I've been set free my God, my Savior has
ransomed me
And like a flood His mercy reigns unending love, amazing grace
The earth shall soon dissolve like snow
Then sun forbear to shine
But God who called me here below
Will be forever mine, will be forever mine
You are forever mine

JOURNEY TWELVE

Discuss last week's homework.

Statement of Truth:

The choices you make, whether good or bad, do affect others in your life.

Journey Twelve: Choices

Now that we are at the end of the journey of this study, one question comes to mind to ask yourself if you haven't done so already. Are you ready to choose God and be set free, or are you going to stay in your sin and suffer?_Let us take a look at some of the characters in the Bible and the choices they made.

I know we talked about Adam and Eve earlier in this study, but they were the first to make a choice that affects us even today (see Genesis 3).

> So Lot chose for himself the whole plain of the Jordan and set out toward the east. The two men parted company: Abram lived in the land of Canaan, while

Lot lived among the cities of the plain and pitched his tents near Sodom. (Genesis 13:11–12)

Even God made choices for us too.

Blessed is the nation whose God is the Lord, the people he **chose** for his inheritance. (Psalm 33:12)

You did not **choose** me, but I chose you and appointed you to go and bear fruit—fruit that will last. Then the Father will give you whatever you ask in my name. This is my command: Love each other. (John 15:16–17)

But God chose the foolish things of the world to shame the wise; God chose the weak things of the world to shame the strong. He chose the lowly things of this world and the despised things—and the things that are not—to nullify the things that are, so that no one may boast before him. (1 Corinthians 1:27–29)

For he chose us in him before the creation of the world to be holy and blameless in his sight. (Ephesians 1:4)

But we ought always to thank God for you, brothers loved by the Lord, because from the beginning God chose you to be saved through the sanctifying work of the Spirit and through belief in the truth. (2 Thessalonians 2:13)

"Martha, Martha," the Lord answered, "you are worried and upset about many things, but only one thing is needed." Mary has chosen what is better, and it will not be taken away from her." (Luke 10:41–42)

"If the world hates you, keep in mind that it hated me first. If you belonged to the world, it would love you as its own. As it is, you do not belong to the world, but I have **chosen** you out of the world. That is why the world hates you. (John 15:18–19)

But with the precious blood of Christ, a lamb without blemish or defect. He was **chosen** before the creation of the world but was revealed in these last times for your sake. (1 Peter 1:19–20)

But you are a **chosen** people, a royal priesthood, a holy nation, a people belonging to God, that you may declare the praises of him who called you out of darkness into his wonderful light. (1 Peter 2:9)

What choices through the addiction of pornography do you regret? Take ten minutes and write your answers below and discuss.

_____

_____

_____

_____

_____

_____

_____

_____

_____

_____

_____

Jesus answered, "My teaching is not my own. It comes from him who sent me. If anyone **chooses** to do God's will, he will find out whether my teaching comes from God or whether I speak on my own. (John 7:16–17)

Choose my instruction instead of silver, knowledge rather than **choice** gold. Proverbs 8:10. How much better to get wisdom than gold, to choose understanding rather than silver. (Proverbs 16:16)

But if serving the Lord seems undesirable to you, then choose for yourselves this day whom you will serve, whether the gods your forefathers served beyond the River, or the gods of the Amorites, in whose land you are living. But as for me and my household, we will serve the Lord." (Joshua 24:15)

This day I call heaven and earth as witnesses against you that I have set before you life and death, blessings and curses. Now **choose** life, so that you and your children may live and that you may love the Lord your God, listen to his voice, and hold fast to him. For the Lord is your life, and he will give you many years in the land he swore to give to your fathers, Abraham, Isaac, and Jacob. (Deuteronomy 30:19–20)

More of my story: When God talked to me in church that day about my addiction, and when Pastor Jim prayed over me, I chose to let God work in me and not let Satan have his way with me. It was not an easy thing to do, but if I hadn't made that choice, I would have lost my marriage, or worse. God found a way to use me to reach out to those who are still in need of freedom.

What choices do you still have to make to be set free from pornography? Do you need to get rid of more fear? Pray more; be prayed over. Here is a list of some choices you can incorporate into your daily routine.

- Choose to be committed to honoring Jesus Christ through worship, prayer, reading God's Word, and obeying God's Word in the power of the Holy Spirit.
- Choose to be committed to pursuing vital relationships with a few other men, understanding that you need brothers to help you stay accountable.
- Choose to be committed to practicing spiritual, moral, ethical, and sexual purity.
- Choose to be committed to building strong marriages and families through love, protection, and biblical values.
- Choose to be committed to supporting the mission of your church by honoring and praying for its pastor and by actively giving him time and resources.
- Choose to be committed to reaching beyond any racial and denominational barriers to demonstrate the power of biblical unity.
- Choose to be committed to influencing the world, being obedient to the Great Commandment: "Love the Lord your God with all your heart and with all your soul and with all your mind and with all your strength Love your neighbor as yourself" (Mark 12:30–31).
- Choose to be committed to sexual purity in marriage.
- Choose to be committed to being honest and truthful.

Design a plan that will help you in this daily battle to fight off temptation and other evil spirits that try so hard to get you to relapse back to porn. Make sure you write this plan down and share it with one or more accountability partners; this will help you stick with your plan and even refine the plan to make it easier to follow.

CONCLUSION

To be set free from the chains of pornography, you must first admit you have a sin that must be dealt with and want to seek God's grace through his love for you. It can be done, but we can't do it alone; this is a spiritual battle that you and I can't fight and win on our own. As it says in James 4:7, "Submit yourselves, then, to God. Resist the devil, and he will flee from you." We were set free from our sins when Christ died on the cross and shed his blood for all us.

Continue to refer back to this study guide for help, or retake this class if you feel the need to do so. If you need further counseling, make sure it comes from a solid Christian counselor. Remember, you are a member of Christ's body (see 1 Corinthians 12:27), and you have direct access to God through the Holy Spirit (see Ephesians 2:18).

Other vital parts of keeping the chains of pornography off of you are your accountability partners; continue to use them, and keep building on those relationships. This is a daily battle for us, and we can use all the help we can get, so stay focused on God and not on pornography.

Don't let the world influence you; you influence the world through our Lord and Savior Jesus Christ!

And of course, one of the most important gifts we have to build a close relationship with God is prayer. But be patient. If God does not answer your prayers right away, don't give up; he will answer you in his timing, not ours.

Last, but not least, use the armor of God as explained in Ephesians 6:10–18; I have mentioned this over and over, and I can't stress enough that this prayer does work. If it didn't, God would not have included it in his words.

Remember, men, this is a battle and a war, and we need to win both through Jesus Christ!